GREAT LEADERS and THINKERS
of ~Ancient Greece~

by Megan Cooley Peterson

raintree
a Capstone company — publishers for children

Raintree is an imprint of Capstone Global Library Limited, a company incorporated in England and Wales having its registered office at 264 Banbury Road, Oxford, OX2 7DY – Registered company number: 6695582

www.raintree.co.uk
myorders@raintree.co.uk

Edited by Aaron Sautter
Designed by Bobbie Nuytten
Picture research by Svetlana Zhurkin
Production by Jennifer Walker

ISBN 978 1 4747 1747 2
19 18 17 16 15
10 9 8 7 6 5 4 3 2 1

British Library Cataloguing in Publication Data
A full catalogue record for this book is available from the British Library.

Photo Credits
Getty Images: Kean Collection, 13, UIG, 8; iStockphotos: HultonArchive, 20; Newscom: akg-images, 7, 17, akg-images/Peter Connolly, 9, 19, Image Broker/BAO, 15; Shutterstock: Ensuper (paper), back cover and throughout, Georgy Markov, 6, ilolab (grunge background), cover, 1, Kamira, back cover (bottom right), 21, Lefteris Papaulakis, 11, marcokenya, cover (right), 1, Maxim Kostenko (background), 2 and throughout, mexrix, 5 (back), Nick Pavlakis, cover (left), 14, 16, Renata Sedmakova, 12, Roberto Castillo (column), back cover and throughout, Vladislav Gurfinkel, 10; SuperStock, 18; XNR Productions, 5 (map)

We would like to thank Jonathan M. Hall, professor at the University of Chicago, for his invaluable help in the preparation of this book.

Every effort has been made to contact copyright holders of material reproduced in this book. Any omissions will be rectified in subsequent printings if notice is given to the publisher.

All the internet addresses (URLs) given in this book were valid at the time of going to press. However, due to the dynamic nature of the internet, some addresses may have changed, or sites may have changed or ceased to exist since publication. While the author and publisher regret any inconvenience this may cause readers, no responsibility for any such changes can be accepted by either the author or the publisher.

Printed and bound in China.

CONTENTS

MAKING THE MODERN WORLD

Think about the last film you saw at the cinema. Can you imagine our world without films or plays? What would life be like if people couldn't go to university or vote in elections? We can enjoy these things today thanks to ancient Greek leaders and thinkers. These people created the beginnings of modern science, **philosophy** and **democracy**. Meet some of the ancient Greeks who helped shape our world.

philosophy study of truth and knowledge
democracy type of government in which the people make decisions by voting

4

Ancient Greece, around 400 BC

• city state (a city that is independent and is not part of a country)

Macedonia

Illyria

Mt. Olympus ▲

Epirus

Thessaly

Aegean Sea

Lesbos

Euboea

Delphi •

Thebes •

Attica

Corinth •

• Athens

Olympia •

• Argos

Peloponnesus

• Sparta

Rhodes

N
W • E
S

0   90 miles

0   90 kilometers

Crete

Mediterranean Sea

HOMER

The ancient Greeks enjoyed telling stories. The poet Homer created the famous poems the *Iliad* and the *Odyssey*. These **epic** poems describe a war between Greece and nearby Troy. We don't know if the Trojan War really happened. It might be a **myth**.

Homer's poems feature many Greek gods and goddesses. The Greeks often studied his poems to learn more about their gods.

Homer's epic poems were often performed for an audience.

epic relating to a long story about heroic adventures and great battles

myth story told by people in ancient times; myths often tried to explain natural events

THEMISTOCLES

(528–463 BC)

During the Persian Wars (492–479 BC), the Persian **Empire** took over several Greek city states. But General Themistocles (the-MISS-tuh-klees) of Athens had a plan to fight back. He built a strong navy of 200 ships. He then lured the Persian navy into a narrow **channel** near Athens. The Greek navy surprised and destroyed many of the Persian ships. Themistocles is remembered as one of ancient Greece's greatest military leaders.

empire large territory ruled by a powerful leader

channel narrow stretch of water between two areas of land

PERICLES
(495–429 BC)

Pericles (PE-ruh-klees) is often called the greatest leader of ancient Athens. The people elected him at least 20 times. Pericles helped shape democracy in Athens during his 30-year rule. Pericles' greatest success was leading the building of the Acropolis. This group of **temples** sits on a hill, overlooking Athens. Though damaged, the buildings still stand today.

the Acropolis of Athens

temple building used for worship

HERODOTUS

(485–420 BC)

Herodotus (huh-ROD-uh-tuhss) is often called the father of history. He travelled throughout Greece, the Middle East and North Africa. Herodotus did a lot of research during his travels. He met many people and learnt about their culture and history. He made sure he knew historical facts before writing about what he had learnt.

FACT:

Herodotus wrote a history of the Persian Wars called *The Histories*. Much of what we know about the Persian Wars comes from his writings.

Herodotus reads *The Histories* to a crowd of people.

PHIDIAS (490–425 BC)

Phidias, the Greek **sculptor**, created one of the Seven Wonders of the Ancient World. He built a statue of the god Zeus, seated on a throne. Made of ivory and gold, the statue was 14 metres (45 feet) tall. Phidias also designed and oversaw the building of the Parthenon. This temple to the goddess Athena was part of the Acropolis in Athens. It still stands today as one of the world's most famous buildings.

sculptor person who creates art by carving stone, wood or other materials

the Parthenon

Phidias' statue of Zeus, king of the gods

PLATO (427-347 BC)

Plato was one of history's greatest philosophers. He had new ideas for how nations should be run. Plato wrote about these ideas in *The Republic*.

He thought the country should be divided into three groups of people. Philosophers would run government. Warriors would keep people safe. And producers would grow food and build things people needed.

Plato taught at the Academy for 40 years.

PLATO'S GREATEST STUDENT

Plato also taught at the Academy, which he started in 387 BC. It was one of history's first schools of higher learning. The great Greek scientist, Aristotle, studied under Plato at the Academy for nearly 20 years. Aristotle was one of the first scientists to study plants, animals and **physics**. His teachings guided scientists' thinking for about 2,000 years.

physics science that studies matter, energy, force and motion

ALEXANDER THE GREAT

(356-323 BC)

Alexander the Great was king of Macedonia, which controlled Greece at that time. He led his powerful army into many battles. Alexander created the largest empire the world had ever seen. It stretched nearly 4,800 kilometres (3,000 miles), from Greece to India. Alexander built many cities and introduced Greek **culture** to the people he ruled over.

culture people's way of life, ideas, customs and traditions

THE SEARCH FOR ALEXANDER'S TOMB

When Alexander died, he was buried in Memphis, Egypt. His body was later moved to Alexandria, Egypt. As the city grew, Alexander's tomb was forgotten. There have been hundreds of searches for his tomb. But no one has ever found it.

Alexander led his huge army to defeat the Persian Empire in 330 BC.

ARCHIMEDES

(287-211 BC)

Scientist Archimedes (ah-kuh-MEE-dees) made history when he got into the bath one day. As he lowered himself into the water, some spilt out. Archimedes discovered that the spilt water equalled the **volume** of his body. Today, we call his discovery Archimedes' Principle. Archimedes also invented the **pulley** and a screw pump that lifts water. These inventions are still used today.

volume amount of space taken up by an object
pulley grooved wheel turned by a rope, belt or chain that often moves heavy objects

Timeline of ancient Greece

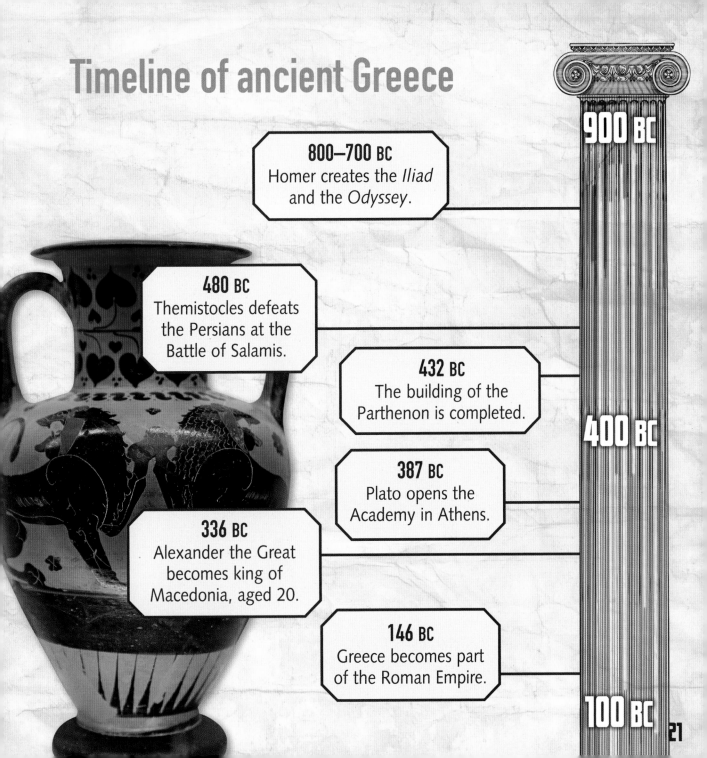

900 BC

800–700 BC
Homer creates the *Iliad* and the *Odyssey*.

480 BC
Themistocles defeats the Persians at the Battle of Salamis.

432 BC
The building of the Parthenon is completed.

400 BC

387 BC
Plato opens the Academy in Athens.

336 BC
Alexander the Great becomes king of Macedonia, aged 20.

146 BC
Greece becomes part of the Roman Empire.

100 BC

Glossary

channel narrow stretch of water between two areas of land

city state city that is independent and is not part of a country

culture people's way of life, ideas, customs and traditions

democracy type of government in which the people make decisions by voting

empire large territory ruled by a powerful leader

epic relating to a long story about heroic adventures and great battles

myth story told by people in ancient times; myths often tried to explain natural events

philosophy study of truth and knowledge

physics science that studies matter, energy, force and motion

pulley grooved wheel turned by a rope, belt or chain that often moves heavy objects

sculptor person who creates art by carving stone, wood or other materials

temple building used for worship

volume amount of space taken up by an object

Read more

Children's Book of Philosophy, Sarah Tomley (DK Publishing, 2015)

Greek Myths and Legends (All About Myths), Jilly Hunt (Raintree, 2013)

You Wouldn't Want to be a Slave in Ancient Greece!: A Life You'd Rather Not Have (You Wouldn't Want To), Fiona Macdonald (Franklin Watts, 2014)

Websites

www.ancientgreece.co.uk
Learn all about ancient Greece on The British Museum website.

www.bbc.co.uk/history/anicent/greeks/
Explore topics about the ancient Greeks, such as the Olympic Games, theatres and gods.

Comprehension questions

1. Many things we know today about science and democracy began in ancient Greece. What are some ways ancient Greek leaders and thinkers helped shape our modern world? Use examples from the text to support your answer.

2. Page 16 describes Plato's ideas about dividing a country's people into three different groups. Do you think his ideas would work in today's world? Explain your answer.

Index